IDEAS IN

Free Association

Christopher Bollas

Series editor: Ivan Ward

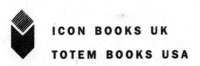

ICON BOOKS UK

TOTEM BOOKS USA

Published in the UK in 2002
by Icon Books Ltd., Grange Road,
Duxford, Cambridge CB2 4QF
E-mail: info@iconbooks.co.uk
www.iconbooks.co.uk

Published in the USA in 2002
by Totem Books
Inquiries to: Icon Books Ltd.,
Grange Road, Duxford
Cambridge CB2 4QF, UK

Sold in the UK, Europe, South Africa
and Asia by Faber and Faber Ltd.,
3 Queen Square, London WC1N 3AU
or their agents

Distributed to the trade in the USA
by National Book Network Inc.,
4720 Boston Way, Lanham,
Maryland 20706

Distributed in the UK, Europe,
South Africa and Asia by
Macmillan Distribution Ltd.,
Houndmills, Basingstoke RG21 6XS

Distributed in Canada by
Penguin Books Canada,
10 Alcorn Avenue, Suite 300,
Toronto, Ontario M4V 3B2

Published in Australia in 2002
by Allen & Unwin Pty. Ltd.,
PO Box 8500, 83 Alexander Street,
Crows Nest, NSW 2065

ISBN 1 84046 352 X

Series editor: Ivan Ward

Typesetting by Hands Fotoset

Printed and bound in the UK by
Cox & Wyman Ltd., Reading

Riding the train

You are riding in a train, absorbed by the sights flying by. It passes an airport, crosses a canal, traverses a meadow, climbs a long, low hill graced by rows of vineyards, descends into a valley choked with industrial parks, winds its way through dark forests, and finally comes to the outskirts of the small city where you are to disembark.

Each location evokes sets of associations.

The airport reminds you of the coming summer and your holiday abroad. It recalls the plane that brought you to this part of the world in the first place; the never-ending expansions of airports; new aircraft on the design boards; the oddity of flight itself; and innumerable part-thoughts that almost enter consciousness but don't quite make it.

Crossing the canal, you think of a longed-for trip on a canal boat, yet to be accomplished, signifying the potential remainders of a life. You think of the Erie Canal in America and the songs and folklore linked to it. You think of your mother- and father-in-law's former house which was alongside a small canal. You might also think of the dentist and a root canal.

And so it goes for the other 'objects' passed along this journey.

Freud used train travel as a model for his theory of free association: 'Act as though, for instance, you were a traveller sitting next to the window of a railway carriage and describing to someone inside the carriage the changing views which you see outside.'[1]

In a sense all Freud did was to take note of how, when we think by not concentrating on anything in particular – moving from one idea to the next in an endless chain of associations – we create lines of thought, branching out in many differing directions, revealing diverse unconscious interests.

For example, when electing a set of associations for the canal, I came up with root-canal work on one's teeth after describing the former location of one's in-laws: a line of thought I won't explore any further, but one which, were I to do so, might well divulge through the process of free association a much more complex story – a story revealed not between the lines, but in the chain of ideas within the lines.

Psychoanalysis concentrates on the daily 'trip'

which we all take, stimulated by desire, need, memory and emotional life.

Trains of thought

The method of free association was designed to reveal a 'train of thought'. By just talking freely, any person reveals a line of thought – an Other line of thought[2] – linked by some hidden logic that connects seemingly disconnected ideas.

This is an ordinary part of everyday thinking. For example, I might start my walk to work thinking about a bill I must be sure to pay that afternoon when I'm at my office; then think about the rainfall and wonder if the sun will come out today; then think about a friend's newly published book which I haven't read and feel I should before we meet for dinner next week; then think about my early schooldays as I see children being dropped off at the nearby school; then think about how worried one could get as a child about being on time for school; then, on sight of a few sparrows flying by, think about the spring and wonder if they are now nesting; then think of the phrase 'nest eggs'. Here we may observe, in brief, the following chain: bills; rainfall; friend's book;

children dropped off; on time for school; birds nesting; and 'nest eggs'.

What do these ideas have to do with one another? Are they just random, or can we discern a train of thought?

I have a bill to pay and remind myself to pay it *later* that day. This is a kind of burden on my mind that may link with the rainy weather, itself burdensome: when will the sun shine? In other words, when will I be liberated from my burdens? Come to think of it, my unconscious seems to be saying, you also have another debt: you must read your friend's book before you meet for dinner. The sight of children being dropped off leads to a thought about being on time: an anxiety about being late that is probably an expression of my anxiety about paying the bill on time; simultaneously, by 'using' the sight of children to locate this anxiety I am also likely to be taking refuge in the notion that a child such as myself should not have to pay bills. The sight of the birds, which I take to be parent birds building their nests, may sustain the appeal of a child being looked after, but the phrase 'nest egg' is probably a way of thinking about the bank and putting money away: building something for the future. Hopefully, I am on the way to living up to my parental responsibilities.

The Freudian Pair

Although he did not 'discover' free association, Freud's invention of the psychoanalytical session gave this ordinary way of thinking a highly privileged and utilitarian space. Most importantly, by asking the person to think out loud, he referred the monologic nature of solitary inner speech to the dialogic structure of a two-person relation, a partnership we might term the *Freudian Pair*. Let us see how he put it:

The treatment is begun by the patient being required to put himself in the position of an attentive and dispassionate self-observer, merely to read off all the time the surface of his consciousness, and on the one hand to make a duty of the most complete honesty while on the other not to hold back any idea from communication, even if (1) he feels that it is too disagreeable or if (2) he judges that it is nonsensical or (3) too unimportant or (4) irrelevant to what is being looked for. It is uniformly found that precisely those ideas which provoke these last-mentioned reactions are of particular value in discovering the forgotten material.[3]

Note that Freud does not give top priority to the disclosure of the disagreeable thought. The idea that the psychoanalyst is after one's dark secrets would not seem to be borne out by Freud's method. Instead, the most valued material is the apparently 'irrelevant'.

Freud believed that banished mental contents re-entered consciousness in thick disguise, and so it would be in the apparently trivial detail that forbidden ideas and emotions would more probably find expression.

The task assigned to the patient has been subject to differing forms of misinterpretation. Did Freud really assume that anyone could disclose every thought passing through the mind? Indeed, would such a discourse not be rather bizarre? Almost immediately Freud qualified the injunction to speak the mind by indicating that there would be resistances to accomplishing this task, especially the arrival of the transference. But over time, psychoanalysts themselves seemed to change the meaning of free association to some form of ideal practice – so much so that by the 1950s it was common for analysts to say, *sotto voce*, that of course no one could do this. Even today, many analysts regard free association as a distant and unrealisable ideal.

Free talking

Matters come down to earth, however, if we redefine free association as *free talking*, as nothing more than talking about what is on the mind, moving from one topic to another in a free-moving sequence that does not follow an agenda. The analyst can and will encourage the patient to talk those thoughts at the back of the mind, or, like Freud, emphasise the need to interrupt a narrative if *other* thoughts arise in mind; but even if patients rarely do this, they are nevertheless free associating if they move freely from one topic to the next in an hour.[4]

Included in such freedom of psychic movement are resistances to the return of unwanted – i.e. previously repudiated – ideas as well as other defences against the mental pain derived from such freedom to think. Thus free association is always a 'compromise formation' between psychic truths and the self's effort to avoid the pain of such truths. Ironically enough, however, free talking deploys the mental process of the analysand, revealing the struggle inherent to thinking one's self.

To patients in Freud's time and today, however, the method has often seemed almost wilfully indifferent to their plight. 'What, you mean, just tell you whatever is crossing my mind?' 'Can't you give me some sort of direction?' 'Well then, can't you give me some questions, which I can answer?' 'But surely you have experience and know something of what I am suffering and what causes it – why don't you just explain it to me?' And often enough: 'Well I'm sorry, but I can't take this Freudian stuff, I have to go to someone who will really help me.'

Psychoanalysis does not provide ready answers to patients' symptoms or lives. Instead, it supplies a relationship that allows the analysand to hear from his or her own unconscious life, and Freud's insistence that the most valued material is to be found in the seemingly irrelevant – a kind of trivial pursuit – worked from modernist assumptions that to comprehend an object (a historical period, a novel, a person) one must study it in its ordinary sense, not pre-judged by hierarchical assumptions. If we see the belief in the quotidian as a valued source of human truth beginning in the Renaissance, continuing through Romanticism's privileging of ordinary human lives, and continuing to this day in those academic studies that believe everyday data is the primary object of scholarly research, then Freud's theory of evidence is the psychology of our times. Even the postmodernist tenet that any truth deconstructs into smaller truths – themselves disseminating through further epistemic declensions to fractions of their former assertions – is an important outcome of the method of free association. In free associating to the dream, not only does the patient provide evidence that will enable the psychoanalyst to understand certain aspects of the dream; but as we shall see, the method also breaks up the unity of the dream into disparate lines of thought – which had been condensed by the dream-work in the first place – now disseminating possibilities that open to infinity.

The floating analyst

If the patient finds the task upending, what would he or she make of the psychoanalyst's job?

Experience soon showed that the attitude which the analytic physician could most advantageously adopt was to surrender himself to his own unconscious mental activity, in a state of evenly suspended attention, to avoid so far as possible reflection and the construction of conscious expectations, not to try to fix anything he heard particularly in his memory, and by these means to catch the drift of the patient's unconscious with his own unconscious.[5]

This way of listening is revolutionary.

The analyst is not meant to reflect on the material; not supposed to consciously construct ideas about the material; not encouraged to remember anything. And why? Because by surrendering to his or her own unconscious, the analyst is able to use it to 'catch the drift' of the patient's unconscious. In other words, psychoanalysis works through unconscious communication!

Any patient searching for an expert with answers

would be even more disconcerted to discover how this 'mental health practitioner' works: caught in the act of drifting, what could the psychoanalyst say to the patient? Not much, it would seem. Indeed, the point of the analyst's task is to dissolve his or her own consciousness by not concentrating on anything, looking for anything, or remembering anything. Asking the analyst what he or she is thinking in the midst of listening to the patient would be akin to waking someone from a meditative state.

Freud's method was so disturbing that even his followers could not adhere to his explicit instructions and their implications. Instead, psychoanalysts have tended to focus on other parts of Freud's writings, especially on his view that psychoanalysis attempts to make unconscious conflicts conscious so that the patient has greater freedom of conscious deliberation. This is certainly true, up to a point. Through free association the psychoanalyst does indeed learn something about the patient's repressed views, and through moments of revelation – when the train of thought becomes suddenly clear in the analyst's mind – the psychoanalyst will disclose what he or she thinks he or she knows, adding perhaps to the patient's understanding of the self.

But the method has implications more wide-ranging than the already impressive accomplishment of rendering unconscious ideas to consciousness: it actually develops the patient's and the psychoanalyst's unconscious capabilities. This, as we shall see, is a new form of creativity fostered only in the psychoanalytical space.

Unconscious communication

'It is a very remarkable thing that the Ucs. of one human being can react upon that of another, without passing through the Cs.,' wrote Freud in 1915.[6] So, when the patient is free talking and the analyst is evenly suspended, the method becomes the medium for unconscious communication. Indeed, Freud had earlier likened unconscious communication to a telephone call, in which the receiver transforms the message into coherent speech. ('To put it in a formula: he must turn his own unconscious like a receptive organ towards the transmitting unconscious of the patient.'[7])

We might well puzzle about how exactly this transpires, especially as Freud – metaphors aside –

does not spell out the terms of unconscious communication. Certainly he cannot be referring to his topographic model of repression, for if so, this would be a theory of self-deception through distortion: how could one person communicate his or her self-deceptions to the listening other, who, presumably, is functioning along similar lines?[8]

Let us search for clues in the Freudian Pair: the free-associating analysand, the evenly suspended analyst.

A sequence of thought is revealed through a chain of seemingly unconnected ideas. A patient talks about listening to Bach's Mass in B Minor; then, after a pause, talks about going to Selfridges to buy a cricket bat for his son; then talks about a conversation with a friend in which the meaning of loyalty was the object of discussion; then talks about a memory from his youth when he found an abandoned car that proved to have been stolen a few days earlier, a topic the patient now realises is connected to a dream from the previous night; and so it goes . . .

What is the link between Bach/Mass and Selfridges/cricket, and so on? Hard to tell, isn't it? If time permitted, we should just drift along with the patient's other associations until we reach a revelation – a point when suddenly we are struck by a pattern of thought, composed of those connecting threads between the disparate ideas.

Looking back, the logic of this brief sequence might reveal the following thought: 'I would be in a mess if as a consequence of my wish to enrich myself ["self-rich-es"] I did not play cricket [fairly] with my friends, especially if I were [car]ried off by stolen ideas abandoned by other people.'

This would inevitably be an incomplete understanding of the associations, however. Certain words, such as 'Selfridges', might call forth other words, so that in addition to the above we may also hear the words 'elf', 'rigid' or 'frigid'; the phrase 'that's not cricket' might be evoked, as might the multiple meanings of the word 'bat', in many differing contexts: 'right off the bat', 'old bat'. But even then, these signifiers meet potential other words on the rim of consciousness. Perhaps you can hear the word 'get' in 'cricket', or the word 'bad' in 'bat'. As the analysand free associates, presenting a field of sounds, the analyst will receive a complex tapestry of many connections – mostly unconsciously.

There is, then, no single chain of thought: rather, as we shall see, multiple lines of psychic interest, moving through moments of life like some silent radiant intelligence. As the analyst assumes the position of evenly suspended attentiveness, he or she comes under the influence of the unconscious order. Guided by the logic of the patient's chain of ideas, the analyst at some point will retrospectively discover what the patient has, in part at least, been talking about.

The psychoanalyst's subjectivity

We communicate with one another unconsciously, therefore, when we give ourselves over to the way unconscious thinking takes place: through the free association of ideas that manifests a hidden order of thought. The psychoanalyst's unconscious recognises this as its own form of thinking and assumes the task of apprehending patterns of thought, some of which can be brought into consciousness.

But what about the psychoanalyst's own 'subjective response'? Would the analyst not distort what he or she hears? How could the analyst be relied upon to detect the chain of associations, given the dynamics of his or her own unconscious?

Confronted with the fact that the psychoanalyst will repress certain of the patient's contents, will condense various psychic materials into his or her own constellations of thought, will distort or alter communications according to the dream-work of the unconscious, how do we claim a capacity to discern, receive, integrate, and communicate with the patient's logic of association?

The problem is one of form versus content. The analyst's unconscious life will alter the patient's communications, dream-working them into unconscious complexes of the analyst's own creation; but at the same time the ego's ability to follow the structure of the unconscious logic will continue, a procedural capability unimpeded by the work of the analyst's own unconscious, much like operating a car is ordinarily uninfluenced by the driver's passing thoughts.

Pattern recognition is the ego's ability to perceive reality alongside the self's own unconscious contents or emotional states of mind. If the analysand thinks through free talking, therefore using the analyst as a medium for thought, then both participants use a part of the ego accustomed to the work of unconscious reception. Such reception begins in infancy, when the mother communicates complex messages to the infant through *forms* of behaviour – recurring patterns – assimilated by the infant as inner forms for processing lived experience.

The ability to follow the logic of sequence is a formal quality of the ego – a type of intelligence – not fundamentally influenced by the internal life of the recipient or the circumstances of the relationship between its participants.[9]

Indeed, in free dialogue, when two people free associate in the course of a long conversation, as is typical of close friends, they create unconscious lines of thought, working associatively, as they jump from one topic to the next. This is easy to do because we are open to such unconscious mutual influence when relaxed in the presence of an other.

Even as the analyst's unconscious tracks associative logic – doing nothing more than recognising the way we all partly think in the first place – on other paths he or she will dream-work the patient's material: condensing words and images, substituting ideas; in other words, transforming

the content according to his or her own unconscious reading. Later we shall discuss 'wavelengths' of communication, and how it is likely
that the analyst's reception of the patient's
contents varies according to differing lines of
evoked prior associations.

The analyst's unconscious knows where it is when
'in analysis', just as a composer's unconscious or a
painter's unconscious knows the difference
between that engagement peculiar to composing
or painting and the many other moments in life,
such as going to the bank or reading a book.
Unconscious perception of the self's unconscious
place is crucial to analyst and analysand knowing
where they are and why they are there when they
create psychoanalysis together.

At this point it is useful to introduce other
factors that have contributed to the understanding
and use of free association in contemporary
psychoanalysis.

Object relations

Melanie Klein and her followers found that when
we talk freely we often seem to be talking about
parts of ourselves.

The patient free associates by using 'objects' to stand in for 'parts' of the self in relation to his or her mental objects, usually differing forms of representation of other people. So the chain Bach/Mass, Selfridges/cricket bat, friend/loyalty, youth/stolen car, etc., could be a free-moving drama in which differing parts of the self *objectify* a conflict in the theatre of free association. In this particular case we might say that the patient puts a solemn part of himself into the mass and then, made anxious by a partial realisation, proceeds to try to remove himself from this mental pain.

A sequence of such interpretations might be as follows:

1. 'You are listening to a depressed part of yourself.'
2. 'You want to buy your way into being a game-playing boy to avoid your depression.'
3. 'A part of you feels that leaving your depression behind is not a loyal thing to do.'
4. 'You will find that such game-playing is just finding stolen solutions previously abandoned by you.'

Where Freud's way of listening takes a long time to discover a logic of sequence – entire sessions may be held in silence as a chain remains undiscovered – the object relational technique is open to immediate meaning. If Freudian thinking holds that the manifest text never bears the unconscious but is only ever a thick disguise, then the object relational view accepts the manifest text as an accurate picture of parts of the self, even if what is being portrayed is open to question.

In fact, contemporary psychoanalysts tend to oscillate back and forth between these two listening perspectives, influenced by each.[10] Indeed, it is likely that the analysand uses differing forms of free association: from thinking as Freud saw it, according to the logic of sequence, to thinking as Klein saw it, according to the logic of projection. Thus in the same session a patient might suspend the sequential way of thinking in order to think through projection; equally, the analyst, for differing reasons, might move from listening in the Freudian manner to listening in the object relational manner.

Special effects

Object relations theory conceptualises another form of unconscious communication: that operating through the transference and the counter-transference.

Patients think by acting upon the psychoanalyst; in this respect, talking is always a 'performative action' – to use J.L. Austin's term – as we have an implicit aim when we speak and we have differing effects on the other who listens. Of course, much of the time the action is benign: the patient is using the analyst's mind as a medium for free-associative thinking. Often, however, the patient's speech acts upon the analyst to gain some specific response, often a disturbed one.

Paula Heimann raised an interesting issue in the early 1950s when she asked of the free-associating patient: 'who is speaking, to whom, about what, and why now?'[11] Margaret Little, although she did not make an explicit connection, in effect asked a set of complementary questions: 'what am I feeling, about what, and why now?'[12] British psycho-analysts were to become deeply immersed in studying how the patient communicates his or her internal world through the wide range of effects he or she has on the analyst.

In one case, for example, the patient always spoke in a very clipped voice whenever the analyst discussed the patient's feelings, the result being that the analyst felt hesitant to discuss the patient's emotional life. During one session the patient complained that he believed no one could feel what he was enduring in his life. The psycho-analyst said that he understood what the patient was talking about, explaining that he was reluctant to explore the patient's feelings because when he did, the patient became abrupt and dismissive. The patient found this meaningful, and said he believed that he didn't want anyone to take advantage of him when he was feeling vulnerable. This led to an investigation of the unconscious anxieties and needs previously hidden within this patient's form of transference.

Object relations theory helps us to see how one moment we may be speaking from our oedipal self to a part of our mother's personality, then talking from our present age to a part of our own adolescent self, before talking to our self in its late twenties. In the course of a week of analysis we will be speaking not only from parts of our personality but also from parts of our mother or our father, each voice engaging some implicit or explicit other.

Listen to the following patient at the beginning of an hour.

Whew! What awful weather. I am completely *worn out, feel like I'm dragging my feet.* [Laughs; then composes himself.] *So, down to work. So...what happened this last weekend?* [Pauses.] *Umm...I don't know really. Probably not much. Saw Frank, who as usual spent the weekend very productively* [etc.]

The patient begins the hour not simply talking like his mother, but having internalised a dramatic, narcissistic part of her personality. He laughs as he did when he would describe her, but he is unconscious here that this laughter represents his amusement over the mother he has just presented. The sober enjoinment to get down to work is not simply a chip off the block of his father's voice. It brings this part of his personality into a typically paralysing position, resulting in the somewhat despairing comment that he does not know: a voice and a self state that was common for him as a latency-age child when admonished by his father. The Frank character is a projection of the patient's adolescent self – a self which typically resolved psychological and family issues by breaking out into great bursts of activity. Thus in the first few minutes of a session we can see the analysand speaking from several different parts of his personality, which are engaged in a form of intrapsychic dialogue with one another.

At times, free talking evokes a theatre of multiple selves and others immersed in a dense opera of identities 'thinking' about something through enactment. And usually such identities are simultaneously presenting parts of the structure of the self's personality: a maternal part, an adolescent part, an oedipal part. So by free associating we sometimes release an intense discussion between the varying parts and functions of our personality, busy sorting out unconscious solutions to varied unconscious interests or conflicts.

Or, as discussed earlier, such parts are elements of the self's personality engaging the analyst's diverse mental processes in a 'play of elements'.[13]

The discourse of character

A person's character is another type of free association. It bears assumptions about being and relating which cannot be thought about at first, but which are always divulged through the idiom of self-expression.

Character is self as form.

Think of a poem. A poem is enacted expression. 'Poems communicate before they are understood and the structure operates on, or inside, the reader even as the words infiltrate the consciousness,' writes Edward Hirsch. 'The form is the shape of the poem's understanding, its way of being in the world, and it is the form that structures our experience.'[14] Students of poetry (or music, or fine art) develop an unconscious sense of the formal identity of the objects they study, so that even if they have not previously read, heard or seen the specific object before them, they can often identify the writer, composer or artist from the immediate formal effects of the object. An end-of-year poetry exam, for instance, may involve thirty or more samples of as many poets, with the student having to match the name to the style.

So too with character. In ways even more

complex than a poem, musical composition or work of fine art, we convey ourselves through action: we enact the idiom of our being through the way we shape the object world – an aesthetic motion that of course effects others. Indeed, the other shall 'know us' through this formal effect, much the way Hirsch describes the operation of a poem upon the person reading it.

We could equally apply a musical metaphor, and say that character is a symphony of the self that uses the other as an instrument to play its idiom – a use the other knows, having been formed to such effect. Such employment, however, is only partially available for translation into consciousness. We may regard this aspect of free association as the movement of the 'unthought known': of something known about, indeed deeply informative of any self's being and relating, but something which must be experienced and can only meagrely be described.

This is *our otherness*.

As the movement of idiom conveyed by any self and experienced by its others, otherness both is and is not a property of each self: although it derives from the self, it can only be experienced by an other. Communication of our otherness is the path our being takes in, or through, life. A poem's style 'both creates the surface and calls upon – calls up – the deep unconscious life'[15] and in like manner so does the self's otherness. If others are open to any self's communication of its otherness – and of course there are many impediments to such reception, such as envy or hate – then the freedom of association that is the movement of character conjures up equivalent depths in the receptive others. As a form of communication in a psychoanalysis, character evokes depths of reception in the analyst – operating in the register of form, not of content – in turn eliciting deeper features of any individual's form in being. Patients often regress in an analysis, living out very early forms of being in what psychoanalysts term the pre-oedipal or pre-verbal world. Such regressions can only occur if the analyst is open to the analysand's character, which inevitably expresses itself through thick movements of 'object use'. These movements operate before words are signifiers: they function in that world when wording was acting something – when the word *was* the thing itself.

The Freudian Echo

Each generation of psychoanalysts returns to Freud, not simply to study the origins of psychoanalysis, but because Freud's writings are so profound that one discovers a paragraph here or a sentence there that will provoke a rethinking of contemporary assumptions. It is an odd thing indeed – and for some quite embarrassing – to find on returning to Freud a future train of thought that was originally considered abandoned by him, probably for lack of time, and by his followers, probably for lack of genius.

Returning to the passage on the evenly suspended psychoanalyst (p. 12), let us ask again: where would the psychoanalyst be while listening in this frame of mind, and how would one know if the psychoanalyst is communicating unconsciously with the patient?

In a sense, the answer is deceptively simple.

When listening to any patient free talking, the psychoanalyst will from time to time find a certain word, image, body movement or turn of phrase striking. The psychoanalyst will not know why this is so; recall that the analyst is not meant to know why he or she is so moved. When the patient stops associating, often the analyst will find the patient's last word suggestive. 'I saw my colleague at the football match yesterday, and he was with a stranger.' Struck by the word 'stranger', the analyst echoes the word. If the analyst is in unconscious communication with the patient, then repeating an evocative word will sponsor further thoughts. In the case of the stranger, in fact, the patient not only talked about what the stranger looked like, he made a slip of the tongue and referred to 'the manger', the associations eventually leading to a fantasy that his colleague had been in the company of a figure who was the new Messiah of the business world.

By echoing the patient's words, a psychoanalyst surrenders to his or her emotional experience of the patient's discourse. This constitutes a working form of trust in the self's unconscious perception of the patient's communications, in which the analyst can subsequently determine if he or she is in touch with the patient. If the patient is silent, or asks for a clarification, or is stilted in responding to the psychoanalyst's echo, this is usually evidence that the analyst has been out of touch with the patient.

The Freudian Mirror

The Freudian Echo is a form of mirroring: the psychoanalyst reflects the patient's discourse, transforming it from an 'ordinary' word embedded in the chain of ideas into something different. The word achieves a higher degree of psychic value, and now it resides in the patient's unconscious as a dynamic force (or 'node') that will attract related ideas and generate new meanings.

As a result of such mirroring, the patient's unconscious *senses* the presence of its counterpart in the other. It is as if a French-speaking person living in an English-speaking culture overhears (or subliminally hears) the analyst speaking French. Thus the patient can begin talking in French, hearing in return the desired language – or, we should say, the language of desire. For this aspect of the Freudian Pair, which opens up the discourse to the permeability of unconscious thinking and influence, is almost certainly a form of desire peculiar to unconscious thinking. Alternatively, however, if the psychoanalyst does not listen in the Freudian manner, then we would have to say that the patient's unconscious does not perceive a counterpart and will not find its desire in the course of the analysis.

Slipping up

Free associating manifests the unconscious. It functions as an ever-sophisticated pathway for the articulation of unconscious ideas, regardless of their derivation: the logic of sequence; the logic of projection; the theatre of parts of the self talking to one another and to parental objects; or the movement of character.

Such increased accessibility facilitates a type of *porosity* as the analysand releases unconscious contents, often through an increased number of slips of the tongue. For example, in the midst of an analysis, one patient is hard at work both thinking about and trying to resist thoughts about her relation to her mother. The mother has always been carefully idealised by the analysand, but by now the patient is well into the capacity to free associate; so in one session when she says 'I shared a close emotional bomb with my mother', rather than the intended 'I shared a close emotional *bond* with my mother', the patient immediately senses the significance of her unconscious correction.

As the method of free association increases the porosity of speech – opening the self's discourse to the kind of parapraxis made by this patient – it is almost as if the analysand's unconscious astutely grasps psychoanalysis as a kind of art form for its expression, and, having been frustrated in 'its' desire to represent the self's true thoughts, rushes into the analytical space with a certain relish.

Free talking is its own form of thinking. By 'thinking out loud', anyone discovers what they didn't think they knew, yet they also find in this form of representation a new technique for thinking. Ironically enough, the aspersion 'you don't know what you are talking about' becomes a stunningly positive quality in a psychoanalysis, where the analysand learns just that. Indeed they *don't* know what they are talking about, but such liberation therefore allows them to discover that the unconscious talks through the self's consciousness and, looking back, can retrospectively be comprehended from time to time.

Importantly, patients find a discourse that allows them both to free the unconscious mind and to hear from it. Analysands 'into' free association are also listening to the flow of ideas;

this intra-subjective object relation (part of subject relations[16]) develops for each person a radical and entirely new relation towards the self. Were the psychoanalyst to be the sole interpreter of a patient's discourse, the possibility of this new form of being (with oneself) would be destroyed. Fortunately, however, analysts steeped in Freud's theory of technique know that one of the great accomplishments of a psychoanalysis is the patient's new-found relation to his or her own unconscious life.

Faith and objectivity

The stereotypical portrayal of the Freudian is a rather authoritarian individual with a powerful set of established truths, just waiting to find the right moment to indoctrinate the patient in the Freudian ideology. If it is something of a relief to find that this is not so, it may also constitute an ironic disappointment. In reality, psychoanalysts who work within the Freudian Pair do not know for very long periods of time what their patients mean by what they say. Hardly in a position to have an idea-in-waiting for delivery, the Freudian psychoanalyst is genuinely lost in the movement of the patient's communications. It takes considerable self-discipline and faith to adhere to this way of listening.

Nevertheless, wouldn't the psychoanalyst be able to offer points of view and personal doctrines?

Any one person listening to any other person can always offer prescriptive advice, including recommendation to follow the listener's ideological edicts. And were the psychoanalyst of mind to do so, he or she could step outside the Freudian Pair to do the same as anyone else. Clearly Freud stepped outside his own method frequently enough to advise patients and to indoctrinate them in one or other of his views of human conflict. Indeed, we may expect that psychoanalysis as a theory of conflict is inevitably saturated in predetermined ideas imparted from analyst to patient. This is a feature of psychoanalysis that any of its detractors can immediately point to, because they know from their own personalities that any self comes with its dogmas. So what is there to offset this unfortunate universal trait?

The method of free association subverts the psychoanalyst's natural authoritarian tendencies as well as the patient's wish to be dominated by the other's knowledge. This is all the more reason, then, to reflect on the extraordinary wisdom of a method which demands that the analyst dispense with his or her conscious memories and intentions, instead to surrender to a form of listening that actively dispossesses the analyst of the ability to impart his or her own ideology – Freudian or otherwise. Instead, the analyst is left with Freudian faith: a belief that if one gets rid of oneself (and all one's theories) and surrenders to one's own emotional experiences, then eventually the patient's unconscious thought will reveal itself.

Freud used the word 'faith' to describe the frame of mind one needed to take part in his method:

I know that it is asking a great deal, not only of the patient but also of the doctor, to expect them to give up their conscious purposive aims which, in spite of everything, still seems to us 'accidental'. But I can answer for it that one is rewarded every time one resolves to have faith in one's own theoretical principles, and prevails upon oneself not to dispute the guidance of the unconscious in establishing connecting links.[17]

Freudian faith is supported by the analyst's intuitive intelligence that reflects his or her unconscious receptivity. Echoing the patient's comments purely from one's own *sense* of the patient's unconscious work is highly productive. Quite literally, this echo produces more material from the patient and in this sense is highly objective (it produces *more* mental objects). A deep intersubjectivity yields its own form of objectivity.

By suspending personal views and psychoanalytical theories in order to support the patient's unconscious thinking, the psychoanalyst not only facilitates the production of more thought; he or she also assists the patient in establishing the truths of the patient's own analysis. The patient will be the author of his or her own meaning. It will be the patient, not the analyst, who supplies the psychoanalysis with fields of meaning, creating a complex tapestry of associations that become deeply informative.

Meshwork and the receptive unconscious

Freud believed that the unconscious was capable of development ('the Ucs. is alive and capable of development... [and] is accessible to the impressions of life'[18]). In the dream book he provides a clue as to how such development takes place:

The dream thoughts to which we are led by interpretation cannot, from the nature of things, have any definite endings; they are bound to branch out in every direction into the intricate network of our world of thought. It is at some point where this meshwork is particularly close that the dream-wish grows up, like a mushroom out of its mycelium.[19]

'Meshwork' is James Strachey's translation of the German word *Geflecht*, which also means 'network' or 'wickerwork'. This 'branching out' occurs in an analysis through the analysand's free associations: in the course of an analysis, the patient's branches develop a network of thought that constitutes the matrix of the analysand's unconscious as it functions within the psycho-analytical space. By asking for free associations and by receiving them through a very particular frame of mind, the psychoanalyst not only increases the network of knowledge but also, simultaneously, enhances the patient's unconscious reach.

The psychoanalyst develops the patient's unconscious capability.

To use Winnicott's theory of the true and false self – a distinction he made in the first place to discuss the compliant person who abandoned his or her own intrinsic desires and beliefs in order to suit the demands of the other – we can see how the Freudian Pair facilitates the articulation of the analysand's true self. By 'true self' we do not mean 'true' as an absolute, or even 'true' in the purist sense of comparison to the false self, as if that were not also true of a person's character. Winnicott meant that any person's true self was the spontaneous gesture – in being, playing, speech or relating – that was evidence of the self's momentary expression of the desire to present or to represent the self's particular idiom. When one stretches, or yawns, or looks at an object, the self may break the moment's convention (doing so while conversing with an other, for example), but such movements are signs of the spontaneous.

True self is the freedom of the self's idiom to realise itself in the forms of everyday living, while false self refers to the self's adoption of forms that restrict this freedom.

The Freudian Pair suspends average expectable compliance. Although it could be argued that the analysand does indeed comply with the injunction to free associate, and certainly Freud was at times very insistent that the patient accept this demand, it is clear that the rule is a paradoxical one. The patient is to adapt to a medium that fosters the articulation of the patient's unconscious: he or she succumbs to freedom of speech.

Free to speak whatever crosses the mind, the Freudian analysand gradually grows accustomed to moving from one topic to another, as events of the previous day, dream reports, self-observations, memories and the average interests of everyday life come to mind in the analytical session. No patient says everything, but Freud did not expect an absolute report. All patients keep secrets, whether memories of differing forms of indiscretion, sexual ideas that seem too private to disclose, or former actions which haunt the self with guilt. What matters in the Freudian practice is that the analysand keeps talking, moving from topic to topic, without (consciously) trying to figure out what it all means, and tolerating the comparative absence of analytical comment.

After a while, patient and psychoanalyst find their own way with the method. Subtle variations in the method arise. The patient will often be silent, engaged in deep associative thought which will *not* be reported. The psychoanalyst will also have many associations to what the patient says which will go undisclosed. Often the psycho-analyst will find that when he or she is making a comment the patient appears to have drifted off. The analyst discovers that his or her interpretation is not used for its apparent accuracy, but as a kind of evocative form: because the analyst is talking, curiously the patient is free not to listen! But in not listening, the patient seems intrapsychically directed towards another interpretation. To the analyst's observation 'you are thinking of some-thing else?', the patient replies that as the analyst was speaking the patient was thinking of x, where x is an interpretation from the analysand's uncon-scious that will be different from the analyst's; but x will not have been possible without the analyst's interpretation constituting difference in that moment.

Freud's theory of 'meshwork' also enables us to expand further our understanding of the analyst's unconscious comprehension of the patient's communications. All along, of course, while in the state of evenly suspended attentiveness the psychoanalyst is engaged in his or her own inner free associations to the patient's material. As discussed, the analyst will often be struck by a particular word or image and on occasion will echo it, an act solely determined by the analyst's pre-associative sense of the value of the word. But in time the psychoanalyst will have woven a vast network of inner associations built around the patient's communications; and that network will become the psychic field through which the analyst filters the ongoing history of the patient-in-analysis.

Repression or reception?

Both participants are engaged in unconscious work, but the co-operation accomplished in the Freudian Pair offers a complementary notion of the unconscious to the one which Freud privileged. Freud emphasised the repressed unconscious in his effort to discuss the mental fate of unwanted ideas. In 1923, however, he was struck by what seemed to be a contradiction in this theory of the unconscious.[20] In addition to the existence of repressed contents, there was also an agency of the mind performing the repression that was itself unconscious. What was he to do with these two unconsciouses?

Freud never formally resolved this problem, but it is easy enough to find in his writing a tacit resolution of the apparent contradiction. The agency of repression was of course the ego, which operates the mechanisms of the mind. It is the ego which conducts the dream-work, which forms symptoms, which stores psychically valuable moments during the day, which organises any and all features of a self's unconscious life. The ego has a vested interest in perceiving reality, in giving it organisation, and in communicating it to others. If in the beginning of the human race such organisation was essential to human survival, in less dire circumstances it became a form of pleasure in its own right. And while repression of unwanted ideas is a necessary defence against unpleasant feelings derived from those ideas, reception of reality is a necessary condition to the self's survival and pleasure.

Freud did not formally create a theory of the receptive unconscious in contradistinction to the repressed unconscious, but his theory of dreams and his belief in and use of unconscious communication reveal a complex assumption about the ego's receptive capability (and the return of the received) in the many differing forms of communication, whether in speech, painting, composing or moving the body.

Psychic genera

Any self receives and alters reality, organising life into memory banks (or 'meshworks') where perceptions nucleate in highly condensed psychic matrices.

Life interests us in different ways. Curious to begin with, our desire seeks its pleasure through countless gratifying moments, memorable to varying degrees. Psychoanalysis is a theory of memory's desire, of experiences that, having yielded a certain value, become the basis of subsequent related interests. Over time any self organises thousands of interests (and their history) into psychic areas that make possible differing new perspectives on the self's vision of reality.

Such mental structures begin as questions derived from simple experiences. 'How can I gain this pleasure again?' 'How do I avoid further pain of that kind?' 'What is this which interests me?' Such questions are referred by the unconscious to differing psychic locations at work on related issues. In the beginning of life, for example, the breast is an object of desire. 'What is this?' forms the paradigm of all questions, and any self will organise a psychic structure around desire and its history that will not only drive further curiosity but also sponsor important mental realisations, or epiphanies, that develop the self.

A patient, for example, has for months been unconsciously working on issues that seem to have something to do with colour and light. One week he talks about painting a room; another week this theme recurs in the topic of the lighting of objects that he considers undertaking as part of a pro-fessional project; and another week he has a series of dreams that, in part, portray interests in the colour of skin. One day he arrives for a session having passed by a bakery, where he noted the pale opacity of a type of French bread. He felt he was in the quiet before a revelation, and in the session, while talking about the summer holiday to come, said: 'I think I would like to go to Tucson.' He had thought of Tucson before, but had never experienced an urge to go there. In a series of fast-moving associations – more like the formation of a realisation – the patient quickly linked up the colours of the desert with differing types of plant and animal life indigenous to Arizona. He then remembered a woman from his childhood called 'Tucson Peg', a woman he knew only as a close friend of his parents, as she visited them every summer for a few days. Out of this complex of ideas the patient suddenly said: 'I remember one day being very attracted to my mother, finding her incredibly beautiful in her bathing costume. I realise that I have declined to follow anything associated with her beauty because it is forbidden.'

How do the prior associations *add up to* this realisation? We shall not know. We can infer that the patient's increased interest in colour had something to do with the beauty of his mother, for after this session he was more specific, recalling the colour of her costume and her beautiful skin. He also recalled a painting in the house – a colourful portrait of a woman – which he had always had very special feelings toward. He remembered finding Tucson Peg a very attractive woman. And Tucson itself he associated with the freedom and beauty of the West.

We can see, then, the patient working for several months on what we may term psychic genera[21] – gathering impressions into one area of the self's psychic life – in order to assemble the mental material of what would ultimately be a new perspective on himself, his past, and his future. Such internal constellations of interest form through the associations of thought during the day, usually in response to discrete episodes of lived experience, following long-standing desires in the self. When the structure reaches an epiphany, understood here as a moment of insight that allows the self to increase its reflective capacity, the person looks upon himself and others in a somewhat new manner.

One of the intriguing features of an analysis is the fact that patients have these organised inner compositions which, like magnets, attract further impressions, and serve as the core of the self's creative articulation of the inner compositions themselves. Psychic genera receive the impressions of life, sponsor new perspectives on the self's existence, and at the same time drive to represent them in being, playing or relating.

Genera reflect the work of reception, which follows the self's epistemophilic instinct: the wish to know. Working on knowing is a form of pleasure, derived in the beginning from the infant's exploration of the mother's body (real or imagined) and the child's oedipal lusts. The work of reception is also driven by the ego's desire for mastery (of its psychic reality) expressed through its organisation of the impressions of life. Areas of interest are collated and stored in the unconscious until such time, if ever, that they generate a new perspective, at which time there is some form of emotional recognition of the presence of a new-found insight.

The work of reception can be distinguished from the work of repression in that reception is the desire to receive and organise impressions in order to have deeper access to the pleasures of life, while repression reflects the work of anxiety, which banishes impressions disagreeable to conscious-ness. Receptive organisations, however, are open to repressed phenomena, and in the example above, it is clear that the figure of Tucson Peg is partly derived from repressed desires for the patient's mother.

Psychoanalysts appreciate that patients seem to be engaged in different unconscious works. At any one time in an analysis, a patient is developing innumerable unconscious compositions; as such, talk about issues in life reflects unconscious selection driven by the desire of each composition. Unconsciously receptive to the patient's communication, the psychoanalyst engages in the work of composition.

If repression seeks to banish the unwanted, reception gathers the desired. And if, at times, what is desired may be to present the unwanted in a more pleasant form, it is also the case that the ego will seek the representation of any of its interests. Outside the analysis it does this on a much smaller scale during the day, when it organises the interests of the day into the dream that night. We can use this as the paradigm of psychic genera. The interests of the day, which in turn are linked to the self's total history up until that point, gather into pressure groups that will urge the ego to form dreams that night. These gathering points are psychic genera which desire organisational mastery in order to achieve the pleasure of representation.

To some considerable extent, Freud provided a theory of what are here termed 'genera' in his concept of 'nodal points'. He believed that psychic life was concentrically stratified, with diverse logical threads emanating from or drawing toward psychic nuclei along 'an irregular and twisting path', and – crucially – that 'this arrangement has a dynamic character'.[22] He then adds:

The logical chain corresponds not only to a zig-zag, twisted line, but rather to a ramifying system of lines and more particularly to a converging one. It contains nodal points at which two or more threads meet and thereafter proceed as one; and as a rule several threads which run independently, or which are connected at various points by side-paths, debouch into the nucleus.[23]

These nodal points are genera. They come together from diverse sources that find in a momentary network some form of shared interest that now becomes 'overdetermined' – an interest now more forceful than before which, amongst other consequences, will demand its representation.

Questions of the day

The curious laboratory of psychoanalysis allows us to see how people think unconsciously. Most commonly a session seems to pose implicit or explicit questions. A patient may begin with a gripe about some aspect of life, perhaps a statement such as 'I hate it when people don't respond to traffic signals'. This declaration gradually breaks down into the question 'why does the patient hate it when others don't respond to traffic signals?', which on further association deconstructs into multiple questions. The 'traffic signal' may divide into 'traffic' and 'signal', the word 'traffic' leading eventually to the patient's anxiety about his daughter spending time with people trafficking in drugs. For a while the word 'signal' may linger, connected to this anxiety, as the patient eventually asks, in effect, if he heeded the signals displayed by the daughter; but eventually that word may diffuse into 'single', 'signs' and 'sighs', and from there into 'sights' and further 'si-' sounds that disperse the condensations held by that signifier. What began as a statement quite naturally leads to diverse questions, which in turn metamorphose into other questions, under the mutative spell of free association.

Patients often surprise themselves with quite explicit questions and – most interestingly – they will frequently supply an unconscious answer. Talking about his anxiety over visiting an uncle, a patient says: 'I don't know why I'm worried about visiting him.' He pauses, says 'Oh well', and then goes on to talk about something that would seem to be completely different. 'I was out with my friend Alice, we went to this restaurant, and you know, I'd forgotten just how loud she can become when she starts to talk about her former boyfriend. My God it was embarrassing.' Following the logic of this association, the psychoanalyst might very well say something like: 'You asked why you are worried about visiting your uncle. Is your association an answer: are you afraid he will embarrass you?'

Chances are this is true: the logic of association is a form of unconscious thinking, so if the patient asks a direct question, pauses for a moment, and then proceeds to talk about something completely different, it is most likely that the next topic is some form of answer.

It is not long before the analysand begins to appreciate associative thought. After all, the material used by the analyst will have come, in this respect, entirely from the patient. The source of truth, such as it is, will have been derived from the analysand's process of thought. Yet the implications of this form of work are wide-ranging and most intriguing.

Wavelengths

When people talk about communication with one another, they may refer to being on the same 'wavelength'. We may observe something of this notion in psychoanalysis when we examine the 'frequency' of a patient's associations. Freud focuses on the logic of sequence in the here and now, a logic that ultimately reveals some close reading on the patient's part of his or her lived experience. But the analyst will also note certain words, images, memories, dreams and prior patterns of thought recurring across sessions. Indeed, it may become clear that a patient discussing the *QE II* liner and the price of a ticket to New York may have had a dream about being on board a ship two weeks before, which in turn linked to his memory of travelling to Santander on a large car-ferry.

Some patterns of free association seem to have large frequency intervals, the line of thought articulating itself over a longer time-span than the more domestic work of the associative logic of the hour. Sometimes particularly vivid and emotionally moving dreams condense issues worked on by the self over a long period of time.

This should come as no surprise.

During the day certain people, places and events have more emotional effect on a person than others and their psychic value will compete to form a dream that night. But such experiences will often possess such value because they fall circumstantially into the path of a prior interest which is now in the process of disseminative movement. Each line of interest is always finding something in lived experience that gathers magnetically to it, forming thousands and thousands of nuclear interests. The patient dreams – often making new links between prior interests – and then the new day comes, during which the dream and parts break up under new free associations and aleatory events in the real.

The free-associating patient, however, will carry on thinking ideas that have been around since childhood, many of which have very long wavelengths, some taking years to recur. It may be years before a recurring dream returns, but its repetition speaks to one particular line of thought, sustaining its interests throughout the life of the self.

The Freudian Pair constitutes a mixed sequential temporality. Although the session is part of some more local interest and binds many prior interests into a shared space for a while, it is also a temporal collage, as lines of thought pursued in many different temporal rhythms are present at the same time. The psychoanalyst's open-mindedness allows the psychoanalyst to be under the influence of any wave of thought, whatever its frequency. Indeed, the analyst may unconsciously perceive a line of thought which arises momentarily, but whose history long precedes the analysis, removing it from any possibility of translation into consciousness.

Does the psychoanalyst possess a temporal capacity that can operate on varying wavelengths?

The repetition of clusters of association, occurring in differing temporalities, instructs the analyst's unconscious as to the wavelength of the 'network'. Indeed, if it is the case that approximately every three weeks an analysand talks about her relation to her father, then we may assume that every three weeks the analyst's unconscious will have tuned in to that wavelength.

Clearly, certain events in life occur at regular intervals. A payslip at the end of the month will always bring up some material about what to do with money. The months of the year bear cultural significance releasing sets of associations, as do particular days such as Christmas, Easter, New Year's Day, and so forth. The analysand's birthday, the date of the mother's or father's death, the date when the patient moved from one country to another; all occur at regular intervals and will bring up sets of associations. But human lives have much more precise and rather dense psychic calendars that make for repetition and create intervals that will not be consciously clear to the patient or to the analyst. Does the patient remember that it was on 5 April 1951 that her mother ran over another child in the family car?

Or that on 14 October 1953 the father lost his job? Or that on 22 February 1956 the patient's mother miscarried? It is unlikely that these days will be consciously remembered by the analysand, but they will have been stored in the unconscious; and when each date occurs in the annual calendar it could evoke unconscious memories linked to all the significant prior events in the individual's life. Indeed, it is often by this recurrence of mood that the analyst will discover something quite forgotten. For example, after working with a patient for three years it was clear that every April the patient became depressed. Only when asking the patient if anything upsetting had ever happened in April did the analyst learn that this was the month when the patient's mother committed suicide. It was possible to observe from the Aprils which followed that the same thing occurred. What is unusual about this moment is that the analyst could discover the agency of the interval, as ordinarily he or she will not know its significance; nor will the analyst know consciously that he or she is on some wave occurring every year at that same time, not to recur until the following year.

To make matters more complex – but more

accurate – we can say that these differing waves of unconscious interest, which permeate any period of free associating, overlap with one another to form the symphonic movement of the unconscious. A patient sees a car accident the night before a session, and as she reports this event it will have activated another set of associations linked to the occasion when her mother ran over a child in 1951. Those will not be the only interests in the hour, as there will be other emotional experiences of the previous day, dreams from the night, and associations before the analytical hour that will have nucleated into separate areas of interest. But all these interests do become part of the same moment in unconscious time, and they are all shaped by the patient's ego into the dream-work of ordinary free associating, in which the patient moves from one topic to the next, quite ignorant of all that he or she is processing in the here and now.

We may well find that, correspondingly, the listening analyst has something in common with the musical audience. For this is an action that demands the ability to follow disparate representations – some repeated, others quite new – occurring at the same moment in time.

The drive to represent

Freud was never able to answer the question that he continually posed to himself: isn't every dream a wish fulfilment?

He found dreams that seemed to be beyond the human wish.

Freud's error was to confuse mental content with mental form. He tended to restrict himself to examination of specific mental contents – anxiety dreams, and so on – which challenged him to find the hidden wish in what would otherwise seem to be a highly unpleasant activity of mind.

What he failed to see was something quite simple: any dream fulfils the wish to dream – thus every dream is a wish fulfilment.

The dream is a *form* of unconscious representation.

By likening the dream to a symptom, Freud noted that the ego picked differing forms for the representation of unconscious contents. Failing to attend to the human drive to represent, however, meant that Freud could not attend to the underlying drive of the ego and to many of the issues that explain unconscious communication. His theory of the instincts came close; but it is not the case – as the classical school was to argue – that all human thought is a collation of derived individual instincts. This is a theory of content gone too far, and it confuses form with content.

The infantile instinct – an intrapsychic arc from its source to its object – is a paradigm of representation. To satisfy the instinct, the self must construct an object. Putting it simply: if the instinct is the drive of hunger, then the object would be the thought 'I am hungry' or an image of something to eat. This is repeated throughout infancy and childhood; it does not support the fate of any individual instinct *per se*, but it does subsidise the drive to represent the self.

The representative drive is what makes the human being uniquely human.

The desire to represent the self presupposes the self's belief in a good object, which in turn is based on the self's communications of early infantile states to the mother who, to lesser or greater extent, has received and transformed those communications. We may think of the pleasure of this representation and its reception as superseding the pain of any particular represented content. Thus the pleasure principle of representation drives the self to communicate with the other, and part of this complex action is the self's unconscious investment in seeking its own truth.

Seeking one's truth

What would it mean to seek one's own truth?

It could only ever mean seeking to re-present unconscious conflicts in order that the representative process in itself (at the very least) might begin to undertake the task of self-liberation. The pleasure of representation finds another pleasure: the pleasure of self-discovery, and of being understood.

Turning to the Freudian Pair, we may now see how the free-associative process continuously gratifies the self's pleasure in representation, especially as it serves the drive to represent the self's unconscious interests. The analyst, in a state of even suspension – unintrusive, concentrating, receptive, dreamy – derives this presentational craft from the constituents of maternal creativity. And just as the mother receives and transforms her infant's communications, conveying through each moment of maternal craft a type of devotion to the development of the infant's idiom, so the psychoanalyst's function within the maternal order effectively elicits the analysand's presentation of idiom for further articulation.

Free association within the analytical relationship differs from the ordinary associations of everyday life due to the process of speaking oneself in the presence of the other. The analyst's maternity, as it were, celebrates this type of communication and the analysand's 'speech acts' reflect the movement of the self as a form in being. Patients free associating in this respect are akin to artists manifesting a deeply subjective style through the form of their representation, much like a poet's signature is revealed not through the poem's content message, but through its form.

This form of reception is surely what Winnicott had in mind when he likened the psychoanalyst's concentration to 'holding'. Bion also points toward this aspect of the psychoanalytical relationship when he refers to the analyst as 'containing' the patient. Indeed, Bion enjoins the analyst to be 'without memory and desire', essential if the analyst is to achieve a very special state of mind he calls 'reverie'. By 'holding' the patient through 'reverie' the psychoanalyst receives the patient's unconscious moves, which will not only yield more information about the patient's inner life and historical conflicts, but will facilitate the articulation of the analysand's being, as a form of expression.

We may now add a further dimension to our understanding of how free association facilitates unconscious communication. By taking in the patient's being-as-form – operationally imparted not just by the logic of the patient's associations, but by the shape created by the speech acts – the psychoanalyst is internally structured by the 'language of character'.[24] Over time, the psychoanalyst becomes familiar with each patient's being-as-form and can unconsciously read increasingly typical features of the analysand's style. It is very likely that this 'language training' accounts for the many moments in an analysis when, uncannily, the psychoanalyst either seems to know what the patient is going to say next (often supplying the next word) or, on the basis of a mix of verbal association, body gesture and mood, can 'feel' the patient's meaning.

Mind expansion

Free association produces further 'spoken objects', over time establishes a 'meshwork' for the Freudian Pair, and eventually creates an unconsciously comprehensible language of the analysand. The psychoanalyst's passing comments are more often 'echoes' of words or phrases that for whatever reason have moved the psychoanalyst, derived no doubt from his or her own unconscious collaboration with the patient. The to-and-fro implicit in this method becomes a new form of thinking, and both gathers together the psychic intensities of the patient's life – from dreams, clusters of association, images, memories – and breaks them apart as these momentary organisations disseminate upon further association.

By the middle portion of a psychoanalysis the patient will have a substantially increased ability to think the unconscious. Moreover, he or she will have been participant in a form of unconscious relating that will have enhanced the self's capacity to receive, organise, create, and communicate with the other. Although all persons form mental representations of the other, in the form of internal objects, psychoanalysis not only favours the representation of such objects, it also facilitates the self's capacity to communicate the aesthetic of one's being to the other. In a sense, it allows self to convey its own otherness.

In some ways, this accomplishment of psycho-analysis is not in changing a person as much as it is in receiving the analysand. And the efficacious outcome of a psychoanalysis may well be, in large part, the deeply meaningful experience one finds in conveying one's self to an other: perhaps fulfilling a need latent for thousands of years in our species, only now finding a form that has evolved to suit this need.

As the analysand develops the capacity to think, communicate and receive at these unconscious levels, then we may say that psychoanalysis assists in the growth of the patient's mind. Although that expansion will include consciousness, as obviously both participants are conscious recipients of the effects of the unconscious work, the greater value of this aspect of a psychoanalysis will be in the development of unconscious capabilities.

Indeed the association of ideas, or 'meshwork', *is* the unconscious. Thoughts, said Bion, require a thinker: the mind derives from the requirement to think nascent thoughts. In like manner, the self's history of associated ideas not only represents particular psychic interests, it leaves a dynamic trace of connections that serve to perceive subsequent 'realities' from increasing depth. The course of associations establishes psychic patterns of interest that constitute the architectural structure of the unconscious.

By evoking set after set of derivatives of the unconscious, psychoanalysis increases the reach and depth of unconscious thinking, and thereby expands the unconscious mind itself.

Psychoanalysis and creativity

Free association is a form of personal creativity. Patients release themselves to speak the impressions of life, not knowing what sort of pattern of thought will emerge on any given day; each session will, in a sense, be unrepeatable and quite different from any other session. Without fail, patients will be surprised by their patterns of thought and the logic of unconscious interests. Yet at the same time something will seem invariant, something about the self's idiom of being.

The Freudian Pair enables the analysand to feel

the echo of his or her being in the method within which the analysand is a vital participant. It is like seeing one's soul in a particular type of mirror. Sessions vary, one's unconscious interests are infinitely diverse, but one's way of composing oneself, one's others and one's world reveal a style that is forever one's own, inseparable from one's identity.

Patients sense how psychoanalysis develops unconscious capabilities, enhancing the articulation of one's idiom through the representational form peculiar to the Freudian Pair. Although this new form of creativity (in being and relating) is intangible and a part of immaterial reality, it can nevertheless be felt and is something of an acquired emotional talent.

Affects, emotions, feelings

The English word 'feelings' recognises how certain affects allow us to 'touch' one another. To feel an emotion and to touch the object use the same signifier. 'Emotions' – the word derives from the Latin *movere* – are 'moving experiences' in recognition of a complex of affects and ideas whose structure is revealed over time: one moves through sets of ideas and affects, the total unit of which constitutes an 'emotional experience'. This may be why people will often say 'I was moved by that book', or 'I found this a moving experience.'

The affects – anxiety, depression, euphoria, and so on – are the base of emotional life, but not equivalent to what I think we mean by emotion. For an emotion is also profoundly ideational, involving a condensation of many differing thoughts and affects, the collection of which forms a new unit of self-experience.

Patient and analyst share both ideas and affects interwoven in the matrix of the Freudian Pair's creation. Such a field of thought and affect constitutes the unconscious field in which analysis takes place and, as discussed, much of the time it could only be said that both participants say what they do guided by their emotional states at the time. But such states of mind are actually complex unconscious organisations of those issues preoccupying the patient which, when articulated through the medium of the analytical method, bring about emotional organisations in each participant. Why does the analyst repeat one word and not another? Because he or she *feels* it is important, without knowing why. The analyst is *moved* by one image and not another.

Seen this way, we can argue that feelings are a function of emotional capacity. If one's emotional life is developed then one has the capacity to feel the impressions of life. Empathy – the capacity to put oneself into the other's position – is a developed ability: one learns how to feel one's way into the other. Through free association and evenly suspended attentiveness, the analyst's emotional experiencing permits a heightened ability to sense the patient, this ability to feel deriving from the cumulative educational effect of emotional experience.

Although we might use the words 'affect', 'emotion' and 'feeling' interchangeably, it is useful at least for psychoanalytical purposes to distinguish between them. For we can see how a condensation of ideas – an important part of Freud's theory of the unconscious – is also a dense affective experience, as these separate ideas would also evoke in themselves a different affect. Gathered together into a unity, such as a dream, the unravelling of this compaction through free association will often involve an emotional experience, if by this we mean that 'moving experience' which derives from the lived structure of emotional organisation. The repetition of such lived structures or moving experiences increases one's ability to feel, which is a derivative of the capacity for emotion.

All people experience affects. And it is hard to imagine anyone who would not have at least something of an emotional life. But some people are so defended against affects that their emotional life is extremely restricted, as is the case with people termed 'alexithymics', since they have an impoverished ability to feel.

Feelings, then, are evolving abilities, and psycho-analysis develops this capacity to feel, which in turn is an important feature of the capacity to intuit. Intuition is feeling-intelligence: the skill any one individual has in discerning something about the other through what nowadays is also termed 'emotional literacy'. If one of the aims of a psychoanalysis is to make the unconscious con-scious, then another objective – or a wonderfully unwitting benefit – is to develop unconscious capabilities, thereby (amongst other effects) developing intuition.

Painters, novelists, composers and others in the 'creative arts' have long been interested in Freud's method, no more so than when they focus on free association. The Freudian technique has certainly influenced the surrealist device of contiguous disconnected images that link in some unconscious manner; and the 'stream of consciousness' novel also plays upon the meaning of sequential thought. It is likely, however, that these formal adoptions of aspects of the psychoanalytic method are metaphors of a more profound sense of affinity with psychoanalysis as a creative form. Indeed, it would be difficult to argue that writers, painters and musicians really use the Freudian method in their work; it is more likely that they recognise something in the method of psychoanalysis that is a kindred form of creativity.

The ways in which psychoanalysis develops the mind itself, the ways in which it becomes a new form of creativity in living, and its after-effects on the subsequent life of the analysand: all are still to be properly recognised, much less studied or given their due.

Mother dream and father thought

Freud credited his patients with helping him to discover the free-associative method – indeed, if we are to believe him, one day a patient asked him to be quiet so that she could just talk, and free association took over where forced hypnosis had governed.

We cannot bid goodbye to this topic without considering what the psychoanalytical method of free association accomplishes simply by operating. Encouraged to bring his or her dream to the session for its reporting, the patient feels supported in bringing something from the infantile relation – as sleep is a return to foetal postures and to the hallucinatory thought of the infant – into the light of day. Psychoanalysts think of the dream as a trace of the mother's body, so to some extent the analyst encourages the patient to bring his or her relation to the mother into the analytical space. Once there, the patient is obliged to report the dream. In a sense, therefore, a facet of the father's law – argued by Lacan to be all obligations determined by one's place in the patriarchal hierarchy – is at work in this reporting, but still, the requirement is remarkably laid-back: simply say what is on the mind in association to the dream. The analyst does not interrogate the patient, or demand that the patient make sense of the dream. The patient does more than simply linger with the dream text, rather borrowing from its form, and talking without knowing much at all of what this means, somewhat like the dreamer inside his or her own dream. But as time passes and the analysand follows differing lines of thought, the unity of the dream seems to break down and the associations take the dreamer very far away from the dream experience. Indeed, this process seems to be a kind of voyage toward many differing meanings, some of which are becoming clear to the patient. The dream as an event that would appear to be self-explanatory is now a dim memory. That oracular aspect of the dream – the maternal oracle that held the dreamer inside it, spoke in the dreamer's ear, brought visionary events before the dreamer's very eyes – is displaced by the dreamer's own mental life.

In this both ordinary and remarkable way, psychoanalysis unites each analysand with the maternal world, yet marries that world with the paternal order, since the patient must keep this process going even as he or she is aware of drifting away from the dream. Every day that this happens, psychoanalysis reunites the patient with the mother, yet integrates the law of the father into the rendezvous, and separates the analysand from the belief that mother knows it all.

There is widespread general contempt for unconscious life in modern cultures, in rather striking difference to the interest in associations, wordplays and unconscious events in Freud's time. Attacks on psychoanalysis are thinly-disguised attacks on unconscious life itself. One of the remarkable accomplishments of the Freudian Pair is both to facilitate the return of the analysand to the dream (and to maternal origins), and to foster a process of separation and individuation authenticated entirely by the patient's own associations. What separates the patient from the wish to remain inside the maternal oracle, or to be dependent on the analyst–father's interpretive truths, is the logic of the analysand's free associations. Over time these associations instantiate the patient's own idiom of thinking, and provide the basis upon which the patient can appreciate the value of the self's unconscious creativity.

Notes

1 Freud, S., 1913. 'On beginning the treatment', *Standard Edition of the Complete Psychological Works of Sigmund Freud* XII. London: Hogarth Press, p. 135.

2 Lacan's idea that the unconscious functions as the true Other – the other within the self – is nowhere more evident than in free associative thinking. The rigorous emphasis placed upon the analysand's speech in the session is one of the most important contributions to psychoanalysis.

3 Freud, S., 1923. 'Two encyclopaedia articles', *Standard Edition of the Complete Psychological Works of Sigmund Freud* XVIII. London: Hogarth Press, p. 238.

4 Some psychoanalysts mistakenly assume that because they cannot follow their patient's line of thought, the patient is therefore attacking links between ideas, such that the analyst not only cannot follow the meaning but also may feel that his or her mind is being assaulted. This unfortunately confuses the difference between links established unconsciously with links operating at the level of the manifest content. If one practises from the Freudian perspective, then one assumes that it will not be possible to follow the material in the here and now on a conscious level: indeed, attempting to do so refuses the very nature of unconscious communication itself. It is an indication of how far some psychoanalysts have

drifted from the original paradigm of psychoanalysis that too many analysts require of themselves, their colleagues and their students the 'ability' to follow the patient's meaning in the here and now.

5 Freud, S., 1923. 'Two encyclopaedia articles', *Standard Edition of the Complete Psychological Works of Sigmund Freud* XVIII. London: Hogarth Press, p. 239.

6 Freud, S., 1915. 'The unconscious', *Standard Edition of the Complete Psychological Works of Sigmund Freud* XIV. London: Hogarth Press, p. 194.

7 Freud, S., 1912. 'Recommendations to physicians practising psycho-analysis', *Standard Edition of the Complete Psychological Works of Sigmund Freud* XII. London: Hogarth Press, p. 115.

8 For a discussion of how the psychoanalyst's unconscious distorts the patient's material and how this, ironically enough, constitutes unconscious communication, see 'Communications of the unconscious' in Bollas, C., 1995. *Cracking Up*. New York: Hill and Wang, pp. 9–29.

9 In psychotic states, or when the patient is not free associating but engaged in a form of resistance, the psychoanalyst will not be able to use the part of the ego that is psychically evolved to follow the pattern of the other.

10 For an interesting discussion of the many differing 'listening perspectives' in psychoanalysis, see Hedges, L., 1983. *Listening Perspectives in Psychotherapy*. Northvale NJ: Jason Aronson.

11 See Heimann, P., 1956. 'Dynamics of transference interpretations', *International Journal of Psychoanalysis* 37, pp. 303–10.

12 See Bollas, C., 1987. Introduction to *The Shadow of the Object*. London: Free Associations Press, p. 2.

13 For a discussion of how free association constitutes a play of the mental lives of both psychoanalyst and patient, see Part 1 of Bollas, C., 1987. *Forces of Destiny*. London: Free Associations Press.

14 Hirsch, E., 1999. *How to Read a Poem*. New York: Harcourt and Brace, p. 31.

15 Hirsch, E., 1999. *How to Read a Poem*. New York: Harcourt and Brace, p. 146.

16 For further discussion of 'subject relations theory' see Bollas, C., 1987. *Forces of Destiny*. London: Free Associations Press, and Kennedy, R., 1998. *The Elusive Human Subject*. London: Free Associations Press.

17 Freud, S., 1911. 'The handling of dream-interpretation in psycho-analysis', *Standard Edition of the Complete Psychological Works of Sigmund Freud* XII. London: Hogarth Press, p. 94.

18 Freud, S., 1915. 'The unconscious', *Standard*

Edition of the Complete Psychological Works of Sigmund Freud XIV. London: Hogarth Press, p. 190.

19 Freud, S., 1900. 'The interpretation of dreams', *Standard Edition of the Complete Psychological Works of Sigmund Freud* V. London: Hogarth Press, p. 525.

20 See Freud, S., 1923. 'The ego and the id', *Standard Edition of the Complete Psychological Works of Sigmund Freud* XIX. London: Hogarth Press, pp. 3–66.

21 See Bollas, C., 1992. *Being a Character*. New York: Hill and Wang.

22 Breuer, J., and Freud, S., 1893–5. 'Studies in Hysteria', *Standard Edition of the Complete Psychological Works of Sigmund Freud* II. London: Hogarth Press, p. 289.

23 Breuer, J., and Freud, S., 1893–5. 'Studies in Hysteria', *Standard Edition of the Complete Psychological Works of Sigmund Freud* II. London: Hogarth Press, p. 290.

24 See Bollas, C., 1974. 'Character, the language of self', in *The International Journal of Psychoanalytic Psychotherapy*.